God loves you. He loves you so much He wants you to spend eternity with Him in heaven when you leave this world behind.

However, we cannot go to heaven in our natural spiritual condition. We are born with a spiritual condition called sin. This sin condition must be cured before we can go to heaven. God has provided the cure for sin. The cure for sin is available to all and is found in the pages of the Bible.

Would you like to know more about the cure for sin that God has provided so you can spend eternity in heaven with Him? If so, please take time to read this booklet.

This booklet contains some key portions of the Bible that explain the human condition called sin and God's provision of the cure for sin. Some sections of the Scripture are *italicized for emphasis.*

©HopeWay Publishing
Gate City, Virginia 24251
HopeWayBooks@gmail.com

ISBN: 978-0-9966890-3-8

Copyright 2017

Bible portions are from the
King James Bible for Today
New Testament.

Some verses are italicized for emphasis.

HopewayBooks.com

Gospel of John: Chapter 1

In the beginning was the Word and the Word was with God and the Word was God. The same was in the beginning with God. All things were made by him and without him was not anything made that was made.

In him was life and the life was the light of men. And the light shined in darkness and the darkness did not comprehend it.

There was a man sent from God whose name was John. The same came for a witness, to bear witness of the Light that all men through him might believe. He was not that Light but was sent to bear witness of that Light.

That was the true Light which lights every man who comes into the world. He was in the world and the world was made by him and the world did not know him. He came unto his own and his own did not receive him.

But as many as received him to them he gave the authority to become the sons of God even to those who believe on his name: Who were not born of blood, nor of the will of the flesh, nor of the will of man but of God.

And the Word was made flesh and dwelt among us (and we beheld his glory, the glory as of the only begotten of the Father,) full of grace and truth. John bore witness of him, and cried, saying, This was he of whom I spoke, He who comes after me is preferred before me for he was before me.

And of his fullness we have all received and grace for grace. For the law was given by Moses but grace and truth came by Jesus Christ. No man has seen God at any time. The only begotten Son, who is in the bosom of the Father has declared him.

And this is the witness of John when the Jews sent priests and Levites from Jerusalem to ask him, Who are you? And he confessed and did not deny but confessed, I am not the Christ. And they asked him, What then? Are you Elijah? And he said, I am not. Are you that prophet? And he answered, No.

Then they said unto him, Who are you, that we may give an answer to those who sent us. What do you say of yourself? He said, I am the voice of one crying in the wilderness, Make straight the way of the Lord, as the prophet Isaiah said.

And they who were sent were from the Pharisees. And they asked him and said unto him, Why are you baptizing then if you are not the Christ, nor Elijah, neither that prophet?

John answered them saying, I baptize with water but there stands one among you, whom you do not know; He it is, who coming after me is preferred before me, whose sandal straps I am not worthy to loosen. These things were done in Bethabara beyond Jordan where John was baptizing.

The next day John saw Jesus coming unto him and said, *Behold the Lamb of God who takes away the sin of the world.* This is he of whom I said, After me comes a man who is preferred before me: for he was before me.

And I did not know him but that he should be made manifest to Israel, therefore, I have come baptizing with water.

And John bore witness saying, I saw the Spirit descending from heaven like a dove and it remained upon him.

And I did not know him but he who sent me to baptize with water. The same said unto me, Upon whom you shall see the Spirit descending and remaining on him, the same is he who baptizes with the Holy Spirit. And I saw and testified that this is the Son of God.

Again the next day after John stood and two of his disciples; *And looking upon Jesus as he walked he said, Behold the Lamb of God!* And the two disciples heard him speak and they followed Jesus.

Then Jesus turned and saw them following and said unto them, What are you seeking? They said unto him, Rabbi, (which is to say, being interpreted, Master,) where do you dwell? He said unto them,

Come and see. They came and saw where he dwelt and stayed with him that day for it was about the tenth hour.

One of the two who heard John speak and followed him was Andrew, Simon Peter's brother. He first found his own brother Simon and said unto him, We have found the Messiah, which being interpreted, is the Christ. And he brought him to Jesus. And when Jesus beheld him he said, You are Simon the son of Jonah: you shall be called Cephas, which is by interpretation a stone.

The next day Jesus would go forth into Galilee and find Philip and say unto him, Follow me. Now Philip was of Bethsaida, the city of Andrew and Peter. Philip found Nathanael and said unto him, We have found him of whom Moses in the law and the prophets did write, Jesus of Nazareth the son of Joseph. And Nathanael said unto him, Can any good thing come out of Nazareth? Philip said unto him, Come and see.

Jesus saw Nathanael coming to him and said about him, Behold an Israelite indeed, in whom is no deceit! Nathanael said unto him, How do you know me? Jesus answered and said unto him, Before Philip called you, when you were under the fig tree I saw you. Nathanael answered and said unto him, Rabbi, you are the Son of God; you are the King of Israel.

Jesus answered and said unto him, Because I said unto you, I saw you under the fig tree, you believe? You shall see greater things than these. And he said unto him, Truly, truly, I say unto you, Hereafter, you shall see heaven open and the angels of God ascending and descending upon the Son of man.

Gospel of John: Chapter 3

There was a man of the Pharisees named Nicodemus, a ruler of the Jews: The same came to Jesus by night and said unto him, Rabbi, we know that you are a teacher come from God: for no man can do these miracles that you do unless God is with him.

Jesus answered and said unto him, Truly, truly, I say unto you, Unless a man is born again he cannot see the kingdom of God. Nicodemus said unto him, How can a man be born when he is old? Can he enter the second time into his mother's womb and be born?

Jesus answered, Truly, truly, I say unto you, Unless a man is born of water and of the Spirit he cannot enter into the kingdom of God. That which is born of the flesh is flesh; and that which is born of the Spirit is spirit. *Do not marvel that I said unto you, You must be born again.*

The wind blows where it wishes and you hear the sound of it but cannot tell from where it comes and where it goes: so is everyone who is born of the Spirit.

Nicodemus answered and said unto him, How can these things be?

Jesus answered and said unto him, Are you a master of Israel and do not know these things? Truly, truly, I say unto you, We speak what we do know and testify to what we have seen and you do not receive our witness.

If I have told you earthly things and you do not believe, how shall you believe if I tell you about heavenly things? And no man has ascended up to heaven but he who came down from heaven even the Son of man who is in heaven.

And as Moses lifted up the serpent in the wilderness even so must the Son of man be lifted up: That whoever believes in him should not perish but have eternal life. For God so loved the world that he gave his only begotten Son that whoever believes in him should not perish but have everlasting life.

For God did not send his Son into the world to condemn the world but that the world through him might be saved.

He who believes on him is not condemned: but he who does not believe is condemned already because he has not believed in the name of the only begotten Son of

God. And this is the condemnation, that light is come into the world and men loved darkness rather than light because their deeds were evil.

For everyone who does evil hates the light neither comes to the light lest his deeds should be reproved. But he who does truth comes to the light that his deeds may be made manifest that they are done through God.

After these things Jesus and his disciples came into the land of Judea and there he remained with them and baptized.

And John also was baptizing in Aenon near to Salem because there was much water there: and they came, and were baptized. For John was not yet cast into prison.

Then there arose a question between some of John's disciples and the Jews about purifying. And they came unto John and said unto him, Rabbi, he who was with you beyond Jordan to whom you bore witness, behold, the same baptizes and all men come to him.

John answered and said, A man can receive nothing unless it is given to him from heaven. You yourselves bear me witness that I said, I am not the Christ but that I am sent before him.

He who has the bride is the bridegroom but the friend of the bridegroom, who stands and hears him, rejoices greatly because of the bridegroom's voice. In this therefore my joy is fulfilled.

He must increase but I must decrease. He who comes from above is above all. He who is of the earth is earthy and speaks of the earth. He who comes from heaven is above all. And what he has seen and heard to that he testifies and no man receives his testimony.

He who has received his testimony has set his seal to this, that God is true. For he whom God has sent speaks the words of God for God does not give the Spirit by measure unto him. The Father loves the Son and has given all things into his hand.

He who believes on the Son has everlasting life and he who does not believe the Son shall not see life but the wrath of God abides on him.

Gospel of John 14:1-6

Let not your heart be troubled: you believe in God, believe also in me.

In my Father's house are many mansions: if it were not so, I would have told you. I go to prepare a place for you. And if I go and prepare a place for you, I will come again, and receive you unto myself; that where I am, there you may be also. And where I go you know, and the way you know.

Thomas said unto him, Lord, we do not know where you are going; and how can we know the way?

Jesus said unto him, I am the way, the truth, and the life: no man comes unto the Father, but by me.

Gospel of John 19:1 - 20:18

John 19:1 - 42

Then Pilate, therefore, took Jesus and scourged him. And the soldiers wove a crown of thorns, and put it on his head, and they put on him a purple robe, And said, Hail, King of the Jews! And they struck him with their hands.

Pilate, therefore, went out again, and said unto them, Behold, I bring him out to you, that you may know that I find no fault in him.

Then Jesus came out, wearing the crown of thorns, and the purple robe. And Pilate said unto them, Behold the man!

When the chief priests, therefore, and officers saw him, they cried out, saying, Crucify him, crucify him.

Pilate said unto them, You take him, and crucify him: for I find no fault in him.

The Jews answered him, We have a law, and by our law he ought to die, because he made himself the Son of God.

When Pilate, therefore, heard that saying he was more afraid; and went again into the judgment hall, and said unto Jesus, Where are you from? But Jesus gave him no answer.

Then Pilate said unto him, Are you not speaking to me? Don't you know that I have power to crucify you, and have power to release you?

Jesus answered, You could have no power at all against me, unless it was given to you from above: therefore, he who delivered me unto you has the greater sin.

And from then on Pilate sought to release him: but the Jews cried out, saying, If you let this man go, you are not Caesar's friend: whoever makes himself a king speaks against Caesar. When Pilate, therefore, heard that saying he brought Jesus out, and sat down in the judgment seat in a place that is called the Pavement, but in the Hebrew, Gabbatha.

And it was the preparation of the Passover, and about noon: and he said unto the Jews, Behold your King! But they cried out, Away with him, away with him, crucify him. Pilate said unto them, Shall I crucify your King? The chief priest answered, We have no king but Caesar.

16 Then he delivered him, therefore, unto them to be crucified. They took Jesus and led him away. And he bearing his cross went out to a place called the place of a skull, which is called in the Hebrew Golgotha: where they crucified him, and two others with him, on either side one, and Jesus in the middle.

And Pilate wrote a title, and put it on the cross. And the writing was, JESUS OF NAZARETH THE KING OF THE JEWS. Then many of the Jews read this title: for the place where Jesus was crucified was near the city: and it was written in Hebrew, and Greek, and Latin.

Then the chief priests of the Jews said to Pilate, Do not write, The King of the Jews; but that he said, I am King of the Jews. Pilate answered, What I have written I have written.

Then the soldiers, when they had crucified Jesus, took his garments, and made four parts, to every soldier a part; and also his tunic: now the tunic was without seam, woven from the top throughout.

They said, therefore, among themselves, Let us not tear it, but cast lots for it, whose it shall be: that the Scripture might be fulfilled, which says, They divided my garments among them, and for my clothing they did cast lots. These things, therefore, the soldiers did.

Now there stood by the cross of Jesus his mother, and his mother's sister, Mary the wife of Cleophas, and Mary Magdalene. When Jesus, therefore, saw his mother and the disciple standing by, whom he loved, he said unto his mother, Woman, behold your son! Then said he to the disciple, Behold your mother! And from that hour that disciple took her into his own home.

After this, Jesus knowing that all things were now accomplished, that the Scripture might be fulfilled, said, I thirst. Now a vessel full of vinegar was sitting there: and they filled a sponge with vinegar, and put it upon hyssop, and put it to his mouth.

When Jesus therefore had received the vinegar, he said, It is finished: and he bowed his head, and gave up his spirit.

The Jews, therefore, because it was the preparation, that the bodies should not remain upon the cross on the Sabbath day, (for that Sabbath day was a high day,) asked Pilate that their legs might be broken and that they might be taken away.

Then the soldiers came and broke the legs of the first, and of the other who was crucified with him. But when they came to Jesus and saw that he was already dead, they did not break his legs: but one of the soldiers pierced his side with a spear, and immediately blood and water came out.

And he who saw it bears witness, and his witness is true: and he knows that what he says is true, that you might believe. For these things were done, that the Scripture should be fulfilled, Not one of his bones shall be broken. And again another Scripture says, They shall look on him whom they pierced.

And after this Joseph of Arimathaea, being a disciple of Jesus, but secretly for fear of the Jews, asked Pilate if he might take away the body of Jesus: and Pilate gave him permission. He came, therefore, and took the body of Jesus. And Nicodemus also came, who at the first came to Jesus by night, and brought a mixture of myrrh and aloes, about a hundred pounds.

Then they took the body of Jesus, and wrapped it in linen clothes with the spices, as the manner of the Jews is to bury.

Now in the place where he was crucified there was a garden; and in the garden a new tomb, in which a man had not yet laid. Therefore they laid Jesus there, because of the Jews' preparation day; for the tomb was close at hand.

John 20:1-18

The first day of the week Mary Magdalene came to the tomb early, when it was still dark, and saw that the stone was taken away from the tomb. Then she ran, and came to Simon Peter, and to the other disciple, whom Jesus loved, and said unto them, They have taken away the Lord out of the tomb, and we do not know where they have laid him.

Peter, therefore, went out, and that other disciple, and came to the tomb. *So they both ran together: and the other disciple did outrun Peter, and came to the tomb first. And he stooping down, and looking in, saw the linen clothes lying; yet he did not go in.*

Then Simon Peter came following him, and went into the tomb, and saw the linen clothes lie, and the napkin, that had been around his head, not lying with the linen clothes, but folded together in a place by itself.

Then that other disciple also went in, who came first to the tomb, and he saw, and believed. For as yet they did not know the Scripture, that he must rise again from the dead.

Romans 1:16-32

For I am not ashamed of the gospel of Christ: for it is the power of God unto salvation to everyone who believes; to the Jew first and also to the Greek. For in this is the righteousness of God revealed from faith to faith: as it is written, *The just shall live by faith.*

For the wrath of God is revealed from heaven against all ungodliness and unrighteousness of men who hold the truth in unrighteousness; because what may be known of God is manifest in them; for God has shown it unto them.

For the invisible things of him from the creation of the world are clearly seen, being understood by the things that are made, even his eternal power and Godhead; so that they are without excuse: because, when they knew God, they did not glorify him as God, neither were thankful but became futile in their imaginations and their foolish heart was darkened.

Professing themselves to be wise, they became fools And changed the glory of the incorruptible God into an image made like to corruptible man, and to birds, and four footed beasts, and creeping things.

Therefore God also gave them up to uncleanness through the lusts of their own hearts to dishonor their own bodies between themselves: who changed the truth of God into a lie and worshipped and served the creature more than the Creator, who is blessed forever. Amen.

For this reason God gave them up unto vile affections: for even their women did change the natural use into that which is against nature: and likewise also the men, leaving the natural use of the woman, burned in their lust one toward another; men with men working that which is shameful and receiving in themselves that penalty which was due for their error.

And even as they did not like to retain God in their knowledge, God gave them over to a depraved mind, to do those things which should not be done; being filled with all unrighteousness, sexual immorality, wickedness, covetousness, maliciousness; full of envy, murder, strife, deceit, malignity; whisperers, backbiters, haters of God, despiteful, proud, boasters, inventors of evil things, disobedient to parents, without understanding, covenant breakers, without natural affection, unforgiving, unmerciful: Who knowing the judgment of God, that they who commit such things are worthy of death, not only do the same, but have pleasure in those who do them.

Romans 3:10-28

As it is written, There is none righteous, no, not one: There is no one who understands, *there is no one who seeks after God.*

They have all gone out of the way, they have together become unprofitable; there is no one who does good, no, not one. Their throat is an open tomb; with their tongues they have used deceit; the poison of asps is under their lips: Whose mouth is full of cursing and bitterness: Their feet are swift to shed blood: Destruction and misery are in their ways: And the way of peace they have not known: There is no fear of God before their eyes.

Now we know that whatever the law says, it says to those who are under the law: so that every mouth may be stopped and the whole world may become guilty before God.

Therefore, by the deeds of the law there shall no flesh be justified in his sight: for by the law is the knowledge of sin. But now the righteousness of God without the law is revealed, being witnessed by the law and the prophets; Even the righteousness of God which is by faith in Jesus Christ unto all and upon all those who believe: for there is no difference: *For all have sinned and come short of the glory of God; Being justified freely by his grace through the redemption that is in Christ Jesus: Whom God has set forth to be a propitiation through faith in his blood, to declare his righteousness for the remission of sins that are past, through the forbearance of God; To declare, I say, at this time his righteousness: that he might be just and the justifier of him who believes in Jesus.*

Where is boasting then? It is excluded. By what law? Of works? No: but by the law of faith. *Therefore we conclude that a man is justified by faith without the deeds of the law.*

Romans: Chapter 5

Therefore, being justified by faith, we have peace with God through our Lord Jesus Christ: by whom also we have access by faith into this grace in which we stand and rejoice in hope of the glory of God.

And not only so, but we glory in tribulations also: knowing that tribulation produces patience; and patience, experience; and experience, hope: and hope does not disappoint; because the love of God is shed abroad in our hearts by the Holy Spirit who is given unto us.

For when we were yet without strength, in due time Christ died for the ungodly. For scarcely for a righteous man will one die: yet perhaps for a good man some would even dare to die. But God demonstrated his love to us, in that, while we were yet sinners, Christ died for us.

Much more then, being now justified by his blood, we shall be saved from wrath through him. For if, when we were enemies, we were reconciled to God by the death of his Son, much more, being reconciled, we shall be saved by his life.

And not only so, but we also joy in God through our Lord Jesus Christ, by whom we have now received the atonement.

Therefore, as by one man sin entered into the world and death by sin; and so death passed upon all men for all have sinned: (For until the law sin was in the world: but sin is not imputed when there is no law.

Nevertheless, death reigned from Adam to Moses, even over those who had not sinned in the same manner as Adam's transgression, who is the figure of him who was to come.

But not as the offense, so also is the free gift. For if through the offense of one many are dead, much more the grace of God and the gift by grace, which is by one man, Jesus Christ, has abounded to many.

And not as it was by one who sinned, so is the gift: for the judgment was by one to condemnation but the free gift following many offenses brought justification. For if by one man's offense death reigned by one; much more they who receive abundance of grace and of the gift of righteousness shall reign in life by one, Jesus Christ.)

Therefore, as by the offense of one judgment came upon all men to condemnation; even so by the righteousness of one the free gift came to all men resulting in justification and life. For as by one man's disobedience many were made sinners, so by the obedience of one shall many be made righteous.

Moreover, the law entered that the offense might abound. But where sin did abound grace did much more abound: that as sin has reigned unto death, even so might grace reign through righteousness unto eternal life by Jesus Christ our Lord.

Romans: Chapter 8

There is, therefore, now no condemnation to those who are in Christ Jesus, who walk not after the flesh but after the Spirit. For the law of the Spirit of life in Christ Jesus has made me free from the law of sin and death.

For what the law could not do because it was weak through the flesh, God sending his own Son in the likeness of sinful flesh and for sin, condemned sin in the flesh: that the righteousness of the law might be fulfilled in us who do not walk after the flesh but after the Spirit.

For they who live according to the flesh do mind the things of the flesh; but they who live according to the Spirit the things of the Spirit.

For to be carnally minded is death but to be spiritually minded is life and peace. Because the carnal mind is enmity against God: for it is not subject to the law of God, neither indeed can be. So then they who are in the flesh cannot please God.

But you are not in the flesh but in the Spirit, if the Spirit of God dwells in you. Now if any man does not have the Spirit of Christ he is not his. And if Christ is in you the body is dead because of sin; but the Spirit is life because of righteousness.

But if the Spirit of him who raised Jesus from the dead dwells in you; he who raised Christ from the dead shall also give life your mortal bodies by his Spirit who dwells in you. Therefore, brethren, we are not debtors to the flesh, to live according to the flesh.

For if you live according to the flesh you shall die: but if you by the Spirit do put to death the deeds of the body you shall live.

For as many as are led by the Spirit of God, they are the children of God. For you have not received the spirit of bondage again to fear; but you have received the Spirit of adoption, by whom, we cry, Abba, Father.

The Spirit himself bears witness with our spirit that we are the children of God: and if children then heirs; heirs of God, and joint-heirs with Christ; for if we suffer with him we will also be glorified together.

For I know that the sufferings of this present time are not worthy to be compared with the glory which shall be revealed in us. For the earnest expectation of the creation is waiting for the manifestation of the children of God.

For the creation was made subject to futility, not willingly, but by reason of him who has subjected the same in hope, because the creation itself also shall be delivered from the bondage of corruption into the glorious liberty of the children of God.

For we know that the whole creation groans and travails in pain together until now. And not only they, but we ourselves also, who have the first fruits of the

Spirit, even we ourselves groan within ourselves, waiting for the adoption which is the redemption of our body.

For we are saved by hope: but hope that is seen is not hope: for what a man sees, why does he yet hope for it? But if we hope for that which we do not see, then we do patiently wait for it.

Likewise the Spirit also helps our weaknesses: for we do not know what we should pray for as we ought: but the Spirit himself makes intercession for us with groanings which cannot be uttered. And he who searches the hearts knows what the mind of the Spirit is because he makes intercession for the saints according to the will of God.

And we know that all things work together for good to those who love God, to those who are the called according to his purpose. For whom he did foreknow, he also did predestinate to be conformed to the image of his Son, that he might be the firstborn among many brethren.

Moreover, whom he did predestinate, those he also called: and whom he called, those he also justified: and whom he justified, those he also glorified. What then shall we say to these things? If God is for us who can be against us?

He who did not spare his own Son, but delivered him up for all of us, how shall he not with him also freely give us all things? Who shall lay anything to the charge of God's elect? It is God who justifies.

Who is he who condemns? It is Christ who died, yes rather, who rose again, who is even at the right hand of God, who also makes intercession for us. Who shall separate us from the love of Christ? Shall tribulation, or distress, or persecution, or famine, or nakedness, or peril, or sword?

As it is written, For your sake we are killed all the day long; we are considered as sheep for the slaughter. In all these things we are more than conquerors through him who loved us.

For I am persuaded, that neither death, nor life, nor angels, nor principalities, nor powers, nor things present, nor things to come, nor height, nor depth, nor any other creature, shall be able to separate us from the love of God, which is in Christ Jesus our Lord.

Ephesians: Chapters 1 & 2

Ephesians 1

Paul, an apostle of Jesus Christ by the will of God, to the saints who are at Ephesus, and to the faithful in Christ Jesus: grace be to you, and peace, from God our Father, and from the Lord Jesus Christ.

Blessed be the God and Father of our Lord Jesus Christ, who has blessed us with all spiritual blessings in heavenly places in Christ: according as he has chosen us in him before the foundation of the world, that we should be holy and without blame before him in love: having predestinated us unto the adoption of children by Jesus Christ to himself, according to the good pleasure of his will, to the praise of the glory of his grace, in which he has made us accepted in the beloved.

In whom we have redemption through his blood, the forgiveness of sins, according to the riches of his grace; in which he has abounded toward us in all wisdom and prudence; having made known unto us the mystery of his will, according to his good pleasure which he has purposed in himself: that in the dispensation of the fullness of times he might gather together in one all things in Christ, both which are in heaven, and which are on earth; even in him: in whom we have also obtained an inheritance, being predestinated according to the purpose of him who works all things after the counsel of his own will: that we who first trusted in Christ should be to the praise of his glory.

In whom you also trusted, after you heard the word of truth, the gospel of your salvation: in whom also after you believed, you were sealed with the Holy

Spirit of promise, who is the down payment on our inheritance until the redemption of the purchased possession, unto the praise of his glory.

Therefore I also, after I heard of your faith in the Lord Jesus, and love unto all the saints, do not cease to give thanks for you, making mention of you in my prayers; that the God of our Lord Jesus Christ, the Father of glory, may give unto you the spirit of wisdom and revelation in the knowledge of him: the eyes of your understanding being enlightened; that you may know what the hope of his calling is, and what the riches of the glory of his inheritance in the saints, and what the exceeding greatness of his power toward us who believe is, according to the working of his mighty power, which he worked in Christ, when he raised him from the dead, and set him at his own right hand in the heavenly places, far above all principality, and power, and might, and dominion, and every name that is named, not only in this world, but also in that which is to come: and has put all things under his feet, and made him the head over all things to the church, which is his body, the fullness of him who fills all in all.

Ephesians 2

And he has made you alive, who were dead in trespasses and sins; in time past you walked according to the course of this world, according to the prince of the power of the air, the spirit that now works in the children of disobedience: among whom we also all had our way of living in times past in the lusts of our flesh, fulfilling the desires of the flesh and of the mind; and were by nature the children of wrath, even as others.

But God, who is rich in mercy, for his great love with which he loved us, even when we were dead in sins, has made us alive together with Christ, (by grace you are saved;) and has raised us up together, and made us sit together in heavenly places in Christ Jesus: that in the ages to come he might show the exceeding riches of his grace in his kindness toward us through Christ Jesus.

For by grace are you saved through faith; and that not of yourselves: it is the gift of God: not of works, lest any man should boast. For we are his workmanship, created in Christ Jesus unto good works, which God has before ordained that we should walk in them.

Therefore remember, that you being in time past Gentiles in the flesh, who are called uncircumcision by those who are called the circumcision in the flesh made by hands; at that time you were without Christ, being aliens from the commonwealth of Israel, and strangers from the covenants of promise, having no hope, and without God in the world: but now in Christ

Jesus you who were far off have been made near by the blood of Christ.

For he is our peace, who has made both one, and has broken down the middle wall of partition between us; having abolished in his flesh the enmity, even the law of commandments contained in ordinances; in order to make in himself from two one new man, so making peace; and that he might reconcile both unto God in one body by the cross, having slain the enmity by it: and came and preached peace to you who were far off, and to those who were near.

For through him we both have access by one Spirit unto the Father.

Now therefore you are no longer strangers and foreigners, but fellow citizens with the saints, and of the household of God; and are built upon the foundation of the apostles and prophets, Jesus Christ himself being the chief corner stone; in whom all the building rightly framed together grows unto a holy temple in the Lord:

in whom you also are built together for a habitation of God through the Spirit.

First Peter: Chapter 1

Peter, an apostle of Jesus Christ, to the pilgrims scattered throughout Pontus, Galatia, Cappadocia, Asia, and Bithynia, elect according to the foreknowledge of God the Father, through sanctification of the Spirit, for obedience and sprinkling of the blood of Jesus Christ: Grace unto you, and peace, be multiplied.

Blessed be the God and Father of our Lord Jesus Christ, who according to his abundant mercy has begotten us again unto a living hope by the resurrection of Jesus Christ from the dead, to an inheritance incorruptible, and undefiled, and that does not fade away, reserved in heaven for you, who are kept by the power of God through faith unto salvation ready to be revealed in the last time.

In this you greatly rejoice, though now for a time, if need be, you are in heaviness through various trials: that the trial of your faith, being much more precious than of gold that perishes, though it is tried with fire, might be found unto praise and honor and glory at the appearing of Jesus Christ: whom having not seen, you love; in whom, though now you do not see him, yet believing, you rejoice with joy unspeakable and full of glory: having received the end of your faith, even the salvation of your souls.

Of which salvation the prophets have inquired and searched diligently, who prophesied of the grace that should come unto you: searching what, or what manner of time the Spirit of Christ that was in them did signify, when he testified beforehand the sufferings of Christ, and the glory that should follow.

Unto whom it was revealed, that not unto themselves, but unto us they did minister the things, which are now reported unto you by those who have preached the gospel unto you by the Holy Spirit sent down from heaven; which things the angels desire to look into.

Therefore gird up the loins of your mind, be sober, and hope to the end for the grace that is to be brought unto you at the revelation of Jesus Christ; as obedient children, not conforming yourselves according to the former lusts in your ignorance: but as he who has called you is holy, so you are to be holy in all manner of conduct; because it is written, You are to be holy; for I am holy.

And if you call on the Father, who without respect of persons judges according to every man's work, pass the time of your stay here in fear: for you know that you were not redeemed with corruptible things, like silver and gold, from your futile way of living received by tradition from your fathers; but with the precious blood of Christ, as of a lamb without blemish and without spot:

who verily was foreordained before the foundation of the world, but was manifest in these last times for you, who by him do believe in God, who raised him up from the dead, and gave him glory; that your faith and hope might be in God.

Seeing you have purified your souls in obeying the truth through the Spirit unto sincere love of the brethren, see that you love one another with a pure heart fervently: having been born again, not of corruptible seed, but of incorruptible, by the word of God, which lives and abides forever.

For all flesh is like grass, and all the glory of man like the flower of grass. The grass withers, and the flower of it falls away: but the word of the Lord endures forever. And this is the word by which the gospel is preached unto you.

First Corinthians 15:1-4

Moreover, brethren, I declare unto you the gospel which I preached unto you, which also you have received, and in which you stand; by which also you are saved, if you keep in memory what I preached unto you, unless you have believed in vain.

For I delivered unto you first of all that which I also received, how that Christ died for our sins according to the Scriptures; and that he was buried, and that he rose again the third day according to the Scriptures:

The Revelation: Chapters 20:11-21:8

Revelation 20:11-15

And I saw a great white throne, and him who sat on it, from whose face the earth and the heaven fled away; and there was found no place for them. And I saw the dead, small and great, stand before God; and the books were opened: and another book was opened, which is the book of life: and the dead were judged out of those things which were written in the books, according to their works.

And the sea gave up the dead who were in it; and death and hell delivered up the dead who were in them: and they were judged every man according to their works.

And death and hell were thrown into the lake of fire. This is the second death. And whoever was not found written in the book of life was thrown into the lake of fire.

Revelation 21:1-8

And I saw a new heaven and a new earth: for the first heaven and the first earth had passed away; and there was no more sea.

And I John saw the holy city, New Jerusalem, coming down from God out of heaven, prepared as a bride adorned for her husband.

And I heard a great voice out of heaven saying, Behold, the tabernacle of God is with men, and he will dwell with them, and they shall be his people, and God himself shall be with them, and be their God.

And God shall wipe away all tears from their eyes; and there shall be no more death, neither sorrow, nor crying, neither shall there be any more pain: for the former things have passed away.

And he who sat upon the throne said, Behold, I make all things new. And he said unto me, Write: for these words are true and faithful.

And he said unto me, It is done. *I am Alpha and Omega, the beginning and the end. I will give unto him who is thirsty from the fountain of the water of life freely.*

He who overcomes shall inherit all things; and I will be his God, and he shall be my son. But the fearful, and unbelieving, and the abominable, and murderers, and sexually immoral, and sorcerers, and idolaters, and all liars, shall have their part in the lake which burns with fire and brimstone: which is the second death.

Romans 10:8-13

But what does it say? The word is near you, even in your mouth and in your heart: that is, the word of faith, which we preach; *that if you shall confess with your mouth the Lord Jesus, and shall believe in your heart that God has raised him from the dead, you shall be saved. For with the heart man believes unto righteousness and with the mouth confession is made unto salvation.*

For the Scripture says, Whoever believes on him shall not be put to shame. For there is no difference between the Jew and the Greek: for the same Lord over all is rich unto all who call upon him.

For whoever shall call upon the name of the Lord shall be saved.

Example of a Prayer for Forgiveness:
God, I am a sinner. I ask you to forgive my sin through the blood of Christ. I am turning to you by faith, believing your promise to forgive all my sin through the blood of Christ.

Summary of these Bible portions...

1. God loves us and wants us to be with Him in heaven forever.
2. Our sin separates us from God and keeps us from going to heaven.
3. Because of our sin hell is our eternal destiny.
4. Christ died to pay the penalty for our sin.
5. Through faith in Christ God will forgive our sin and give us a home in heaven
6. It is our choice whether to put faith in Christ or not.
7. We must by faith ask God to forgive our sin through the blood of Christ.
8. When we put our faith in Christ God forgives us and accepts us.
9. Because we are forgiven through faith in Christ, we can spend eternity in heaven with God, our Heavenly Father.

If you receive Christ as your Savior as a result of reading these Bible portions, we would like to send you the booklet, *"Six Steps to Living Successfully as a Believer"*. If you would like to have a booklet just let us know. Send your address to:

<u>hopewaybooks@gmail.com</u>

www.ingramcontent.com/pod-product-compliance
Lightning Source LLC
Chambersburg PA
CBHW070442010526
44118CB00014B/2164